LEARNING ENGINEERED
PUBLISHING

FOR MITCHELL CHRISTIAN DICKINSON

HELLO SQUARES!

HELLO STARS!

HELL**O** TRIANGLES!

HELLO MARS!

HELLO CIRCLES!

HELLO STRIPES!

HELLO RECTANGLES!

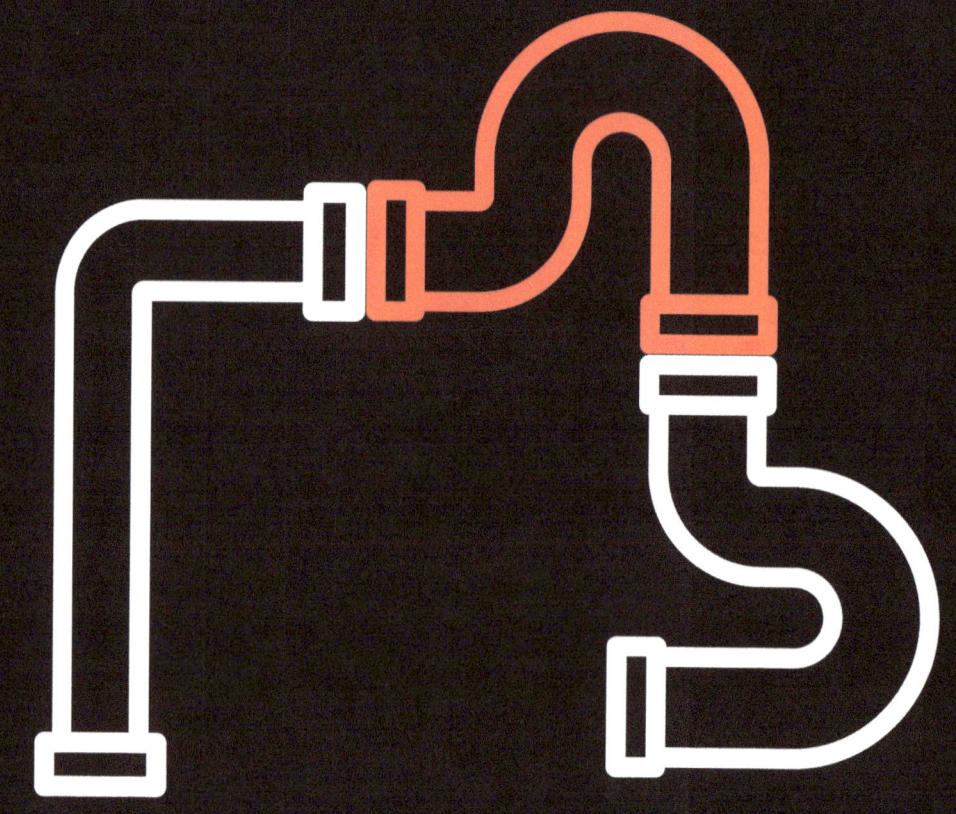

HELLO PIPES!

HELLO DIAMONDS!

HELLO ARROWS!

HELLO CRESCENTS!

HELLO SPARROWS!

HELLO STARBURSTS!

HELLO CROSS!

HELL**O** CL**O**VERS!

HELLO TOSS!

HELLO HONEYCOMB!

HELLO DOTS!

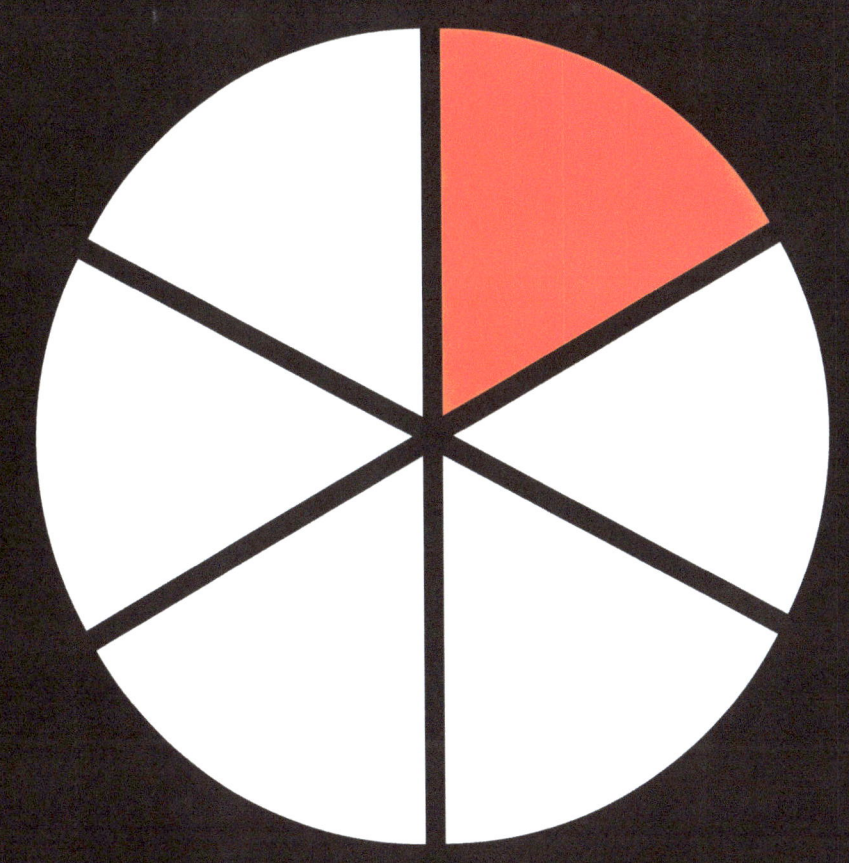

HELLO PIZZA!

HELLO SPOTS!

CONCENTRIC SQUARES

COLLECT ALL THE HELLO CONTRAST! BOOKS!

UNLOCK YOUR BABY'S GENIUS:
BOLD BLACK & WHITE PATTERNS FOR VISUAL & COGNITIVE LEAP

HELLO CONTRAST!

NEWBORN TO 3 MONTHS

From the studios of Learning Engineered Publishing

UNLOCK YOUR BABY'S GENIUS:
BOLD BLACK & WHITE & BLUE PATTERNS FOR VISUAL & COGNITIVE LEAP

HELLO CONTRAST 3!

6 TO 9 MONTHS

From the studios of Learning Engineered Publishing